ESSENTIAL ENERGY

ENERGY FROM FOSSIL FUELS

Robert Snedden

Heinemann Library
Chicago, Illinois

© 2002, 2006 Heinemann Library
a division of Reed Elsevier Inc.
Chicago, Illinois

Customer Service 888-454-2279
Visit our website at www.heinemannraintree.com

Designed by David Poole and Damco Solutions Ltd
Illustrations by Jeff Edwards
Printed and bound by WKT Company Ltd in China

10 09 08 07 06
10 9 8 7 6 5 4 3 2 1

New edition ISBN: 1 4034 8732 4 (hardback)
                  1 4034 8737 5 (paperback)

The Library of Congress has cataloged the first edition as follows:
Snedden, Robert.
  Energy from fossil fuels / by Robert Snedden.
    p. cm. -- (Essential energy)
Includes bibliographical references and index.
  ISBN 1-57572-442-1 (lib. bdg.)
  1. Fossil fuels -- Juvenile literature. [1. Fossil fuels. 2. Power resources.] I. Title.
  TP318.3 .S54 2001
  553.2 -- dc21
                                                            2001000101

Acknowledgments
The publishers would like to thank the following for permission to reproduce photographs: Austin J. Brown/Aviation Picture Library: p. 35; Camera Press: pp. 28, 42; Corbis: pp. 4, 9, 18, 19; Environmental Images: pp. 37, 38, 39; Hulton Deutsch: p. 5; Hulton Getty: pp. 16, 17; Mary Evans Picture Library: pp. 14, 20, 22; Paul Popper Ltd.: p. 43; Robert Harding Picture Library: pp. 8, 33; Science Photo Library: pp. 6, 7, 11, 15, 21, 23, 25, 26, 27, 29, 30, 36, 40, 41; South American Pictures: p. 13.

Cover photograph of oil refinery pipes reproduced with permission of Corbis/Lester Lefkowitz.

The publishers would like to thank Helen Lloyd for her assistance in the preparation of this book.

Any words appearing in the text in bold, **like this,** are explained in the glossary.

CONTENTS

ANCIENT SUNLIGHT

Energy makes things happen. It is the driving force of the universe. Without energy, there would be no universe at all. Scientists define *energy* as "the ability to do work." For a scientist, any activity involves work because all activities involve energy. Even when you are asleep, your body is still at work, breaking down the food you eat, carrying out repairs, and making new **cells**. A rock sitting motionless on the ground contains **chemical energy**, which holds the **atoms** it is made of together. It also contains atomic energy, which holds together the particles that make up the atoms.

Life and energy

All life needs a source of energy. Most of the energy used by life on Earth comes from the Sun. In the remarkable process of **photosynthesis**, green plants and some **microorganisms** capture the Sun's energy and use it to make the food they need. The food that plants make for themselves in turn becomes the source of energy for all of Earth's other organisms, which eat either plants or animals that have eaten plants.

■ Without the Sun, Earth would be a dark and lifeless rock.

People and energy

Much of the history of the human race has been about finding and controlling sources of energy. To begin with, people only had the strength of their own muscles to rely on. Later, the invention of agriculture and the domestication of animals provided another source of energy to draw on, because animals could be used to plow fields and transport goods. Mastering the use of fire opened the way for people to make pottery, forge metals, and cook food. Using the energy of the wind to power sailing ships allowed people to travel along rivers and across seas.

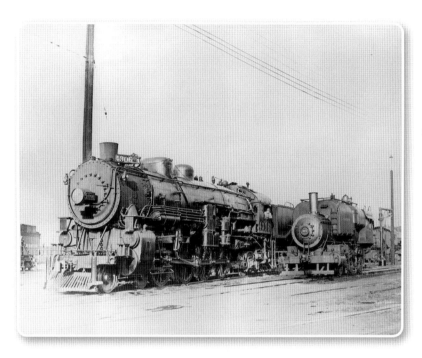

■ This steam-powered train makes use of the energy of the Sun stored in the coal it burns.

With the discovery of **fossil fuels**, people found a new way to use the energy of the Sun. Coal, **petroleum**, and **natural gas** all contain energy from the Sun. The energy was trapped by living plants and microorganisms many millions of years ago. Fossil fuels, and coal in particular, powered the **Industrial Revolution**, which eventually led to the high-technology society we live in today.

We still rely a great deal on the ancient energy trapped in fossil fuels. We release the energy of petroleum in our aircraft and road vehicles. Many of us use natural gas to cook our food. Coal, oil, and gas are all used to provide the energy needed to generate electricity in power stations.

This book tells the story of fossil fuels—how they were formed, how we obtain them, the many ways we use them, and how they affect the world around us.

ENERGY SUPPLY

We use different forms of energy to provide light and heat, to operate machinery, to prepare our food, to transport us from place to place, and to make the things we need. All the available energy we have to carry out this work makes up our energy supply.

Sometimes we can obtain energy directly. For example, when we pluck an apple from a tree and eat it, we are making use of energy from the Sun, which the tree has trapped and stored in the apple. This energy supplies a part of the energy that our bodies need. Often we will use energy indirectly, such as when we burn coal in a power station to heat water and turn it into steam. The steam is then used to spin a **turbine** that generates electricity. We can put this electricity to many uses.

■ The Trans-Alaskan oil pipeline runs over 745 miles (1,200 kilometers) across Alaska.

Essential fossil fuels

The world's chief sources of energy are, in order of importance, fossil fuels, water power, and nuclear energy. Solar, wind, wave, and **geothermal** energy also provide some of our energy needs. More than 85 percent of the energy produced by businesses and governments comes from fossil fuels (petroleum, coal, and natural gas). These sources are called fossil fuels because they formed over millions of years from the fossilized remains of prehistoric plants.

The supply of fossil fuels is limited. Fossil fuels are a **nonrenewable resource**. This means that once used, they cannot be recycled or replaced, and eventually they will run out. Scientists and engineers are working to find ways of getting the most from our fossil fuel resources—and to develop other sources of energy to replace them.

PETROLEUM: Petroleum alone supplies 40 percent of the world's energy, mostly to provide energy for transportation and heating. Most petroleum is obtained from deep underground, on land or beneath the seafloor, as a liquid called **crude oil**. Refineries process the crude oil, breaking it down into kerosene, gasoline, and other useful products.

COAL: Over a quarter (26 percent) of the world's energy production comes from coal. Coal is used to manufacture steel, to produce the energy for steam engines, and to generate electricity. In many parts of the world, coal is used to provide heat for people's homes.

NATURAL GAS: Natural gas supplies 21 percent of the world's energy needs. It is used to generate electricity, for heating and cooking, and sometimes for lighting.

PROBLEMS TO SOLVE

While fossil fuels have been essential in shaping our high-technology society, they continue to cause problems. Spills from oil tankers pollute coastlines. Illnesses from breathing coal dust and accidents make coal mining a dangerous job. When burned, fossil fuels release carbon dioxide, a **greenhouse gas** that many people believe is causing Earth to warm up. Burning coal releases sulfur **compounds** and other impurities that cause **acid rain** and pollute the air. These problems cannot be ignored, and scientists are working hard to search for answers.

■ Coal provides the energy for the intense heat needed to make steel in a blast furnace.

PHOTOSYNTHESIS

Fossil fuels begin with sunlight. Photosynthesis is the process we have to thank for the fuels that power our cars and aircraft, heat our homes, and cook our food.

Photosynthesis is the biological process by which green plants, algae, and some bacteria capture the energy of sunlight and use it to make glucose (a simple sugar) from carbon dioxide and water. Photosynthesis ultimately supplies nearly all of the energy used by life on Earth.

Chloroplasts

The entire process of photosynthesis occurs in chloroplasts, which are tiny green structures found mainly inside the leaf cells of green plants. Chloroplasts are generally 4 to 6 micrometers in length (a micrometer is a millionth of a meter) and are disc-shaped. Each chloroplast contains chlorophyll, which gives the plant its green color, and other chemicals necessary for photosynthesis. Photosynthesis depends on the ability of chlorophyll to capture the energy of sunlight and use it to split water **molecules**.

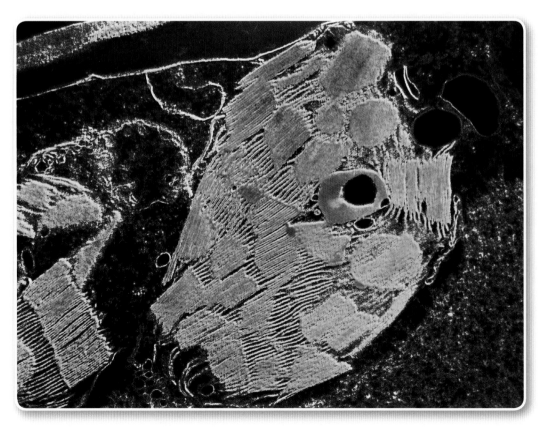

■ Microscopic structures inside a plant cell allow it to capture the energy of the Sun.

The chemical reactions involved in photosynthesis occur in two stages. During the light reaction, sunlight is used to split water into oxygen, hydrogen **ions**, and electrons. In the dark reaction, for which sunlight is not required, the hydrogen ions and electrons are used to convert carbon dioxide into **carbohydrates**. The process can be summarized by a mathematical formula:

$$6CO_2 + 12H_2O + sunlight = C_6H_{12}O_6 + 6H_2O + 6O_2$$
$$(carbon\ dioxide + water + sunlight = glucose + water + oxygen)$$

Most of the glucose that forms during photosynthesis is stored in the chloroplasts as starch. As plant-eating animals eat the plant's leaves, they get their basic energy needs by consuming the energy that has been stored by the plant. Photosynthesis is essential for life because it is the only means by which extra energy (in the form of sunlight) can be introduced into Earth. Without sunlight, life on Earth would be limited to communities of simple organisms—for example, those that rely on bacteria to use chemical energy from volcanic vents on the ocean floor.

AN INCIDENTAL BENEFIT

Oxygen, a by-product of photosynthesis, is very important to nearly all living organisms. Oxygen is needed for us to release energy from the food we eat. Most of the oxygen in the atmosphere has come from photosynthesis.

■ Every second, the world's plants produce billions of tons of sugar by using sunlight.

FROM FORESTS TO FOSSIL FUEL

Around 365 million years ago, during a time in Earth's history called the Carboniferous Period, the first forests appeared. These swampy forests were unlike anything we know today because they had no trees. Instead, there were tree-sized club mosses and ferns, some with trunks over 100 feet (30 meters) tall, competing for light. Much of what would one day be North America and Europe was covered in fern forests. These forests would have been gloomy places, home to giant cockroaches, dragonflies as big as seagulls, scorpions, spiders, and amphibians in the muddy forest pools. Birds and flowering plants had not yet evolved to provide color and song.

Peat

There was not enough oxygen in the muddy forest pools to support the microscopic **decomposers** that usually break down plant and animal remains. As a result, when the plants of the swamp forests died, they did not completely decay, but were instead buried under layer upon layer of mud. Over the years, the partly decomposed dead plant matter was compressed into a substance called **peat**. Peat still forms today where the conditions are right. In many places, it is cut and dried for fuel.

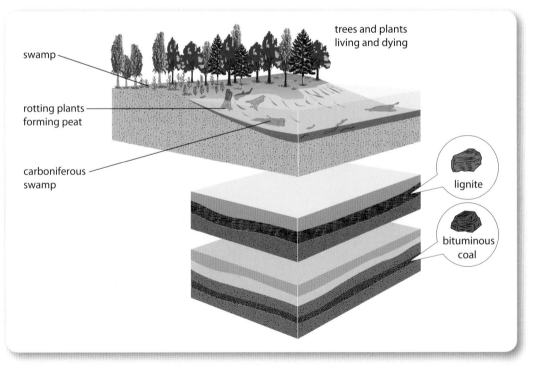

trees and plants living and dying

swamp

rotting plants forming peat

carboniferous swamp

lignite

bituminous coal

- Coal is formed over millions of years as ancient plant remains are compressed deep underground.

Sedimentary rocks

Over time, the peat deposits were buried under sand or other rocky materials. As these **mineral** deposits built up, the increasing pressure turned the deeper layers into rocks such as sandstone and shale. Rocks formed from mineral deposits in this way are called **sedimentary rocks**. As the temperature and pressure grew, the weight of the rock layers pressing down on the peat began the process that transformed it into coal.

Coal formation

The buried peat deposits first produce a dark brown type of coal called lignite. Plant material is still recognizable in lignite. With further increases in pressure, the lignite turns into harder bituminous coal. Intense pressure at the deepest levels changes bituminous coal into anthracite, which is the hardest of coals. As you would expect, anthracites are the oldest coals, found deepest in the ground, while lignites are the youngest. Anthracites are over 300 million years old, whereas some lignites formed from plants growing within the last million years or so.

Coal composition

Coal is often referred to as a mineral, but unlike a true mineral, it has no fixed chemical formula. Coal is chiefly composed of the elements carbon, hydrogen, nitrogen, oxygen, and sulfur, but the actual amounts of each element can vary greatly. Coal is usually classified according to how much carbon it contains: anthracites are about 98 percent carbon, whereas lignites have a carbon content as low as 30 percent. Anthracites and bituminous coal have a moisture content of about 1 percent, while lignites have as much as 45 percent. The way in which coal is used depends on its chemical composition and on how much moisture it contains.

■ These are samples of anthracite, the oldest and hardest coal.

COMPACT COAL

Over 6 feet (2 meters) of compacted plant matter will eventually produce a **seam** of bituminous coal 13 inches (33 cm) thick.

SEA-LIFE ENERGY

Scientists believe that petroleum, or crude oil, was formed from the remains of tiny organisms that lived in the world's oceans millions of years ago. They came to this conclusion because they found carbon compounds in oil that could only have come from once-living organisms.

Oil formation

Millions of tiny organisms live in shallow water near the coasts or close to the surface in the deep ocean. As these organisms die, their remains sink through the water to settle as sediments (sand and silt) on the seafloor. Gradually, over a long period, this mixture of sediments and **organic** remains grows thicker.

As the deposits become deeper, increasingly high temperatures and pressure squeeze the lower layers together to form sedimentary rock. The extreme conditions cause chemical changes in the organic remains, forming a waxy substance called kerogen. At a temperature of around 212 °F (100 °C), kerogen separates into liquid oil and natural gas. At greater depths, where the temperature rises above 392 °F (200 °C), the chemical bonds holding the molecules of the oil together begin to break down. So, if the temperature is lower than 212 °F (100 °C), little oil forms. If it is higher than 392 °F (200 °C), the oil decomposes. The temperature range between these extremes in which oil can form is called the oil window.

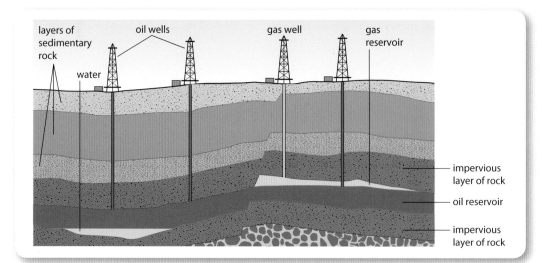

■ Oil can only be reached by drilling through the impervious rock layers under which it is trapped.

Pores and reservoirs

Sedimentary rock is filled with tiny cracks and holes, called pores. Oil and gas travel up through these pores. This probably happens because water in the rock pushes the oil upward or because pressure from the rocks above squeezes the oil into the pores. As the oil and gas move up through the pores, they eventually reach a layer of **impervious** rock that they cannot pass through. They collect beneath it in a layer of **porous** rock called a reservoir.

Some reservoirs form near Earth's surface, but most are hidden deep underground. Although all oil reserves began beneath the seafloor, movements of Earth's crust over millions of years have meant that many places that were once ocean floor are now dry land. For example, more than 100 million years ago, the deserts of the Middle East were beneath the Tethys Sea. The movements of Earth's crust can sometimes bring oil reservoirs to the surface, and the oil appears on the ground as **seepages** or springs. In Venezuela and Trinidad, lakes of oil have collected at the surface.

■ These oil rigs are on a lake in Venezuela.

A CONTINUING PROCESS

The process of oil formation continues today as sediment beneath the ocean floor undergoes the same conditions of heat and pressure that formed oil millions of years ago. However, it will take millions more years to complete the process, and we are using oil much faster than it is being formed.

KING COAL

Coal is a useful fuel. The amount of **heat energy** produced when a certain amount of coal is burned is called its **heating value**. High-moisture coals, such as lignites, have a lower heating value than anthracites and bituminous coals. Bituminous coals are by far the most plentiful and widely used types of coal. They have a slightly higher heating value than anthracites and are the only coals suitable for making **coke**. Anthracites burn too slowly for industrial purposes, such as generating electricity, so bituminous coals are preferred.

Coal is not a pure fuel. It has many impurities, one of which is sulfur. As coal is burned, most of the sulfur combines with oxygen and forms poisonous sulfur dioxide gas. High-sulfur coals can cause serious pollution problems if they are burned without safeguards that remove the sulfur dioxide. Ash, left behind when coal is burned, may also escape into the air, adding to air pollution. Filters are used to trap ash in smokestacks and to prevent it from reaching the air.

■ Native Americans in what is now British Columbia, Canada, burned coal for warmth.

Using coal

In many parts of North America, Europe, and Asia, coal is still widely used for heating homes and other buildings. Anthracites are the cleanest-burning coals, and for this reason they are the best coals for heating homes. Unfortunately, anthracites are also the most expensive coals, and so bituminous coals are often used instead to heat factories and other large commercial buildings.

Raw materials

The energy from coal is used to manufacture a wide variety of products, and many substances made from coal are used as raw materials. Coke, for example, is made by heating bituminous coal to about 2,012 °F (1,100 °C) in an airtight oven. Keeping oxygen out prevents the coal from burning, and the heat causes some of the impurities in the coal to boil off as gases. Coke is mainly used in the manufacture of iron and steel.

FIRST FIRES

We will never know who first discovered that coal could be burned to provide heat. The world's first coal industry was established in China by the fourth century A.D. The coking process was developed in the 17th century by brewers who used coke to dry malt for brewing. In 1709 Abraham Darby, an English ironmaker, devised a way to produce coke commercially and began to use it to **smelt** iron.

When some of the gases produced during coking cool, they turn into liquid ammonia and coal tar. Further processing can produce a light oil from some of the other gases. Ammonia, coal tar, and light oil are used to make such products as drugs, dyes, and fertilizers. Coal tar is also used for roofing and road surfacing.

Coal gas is also produced in coking. This burns like natural gas, but it has a lower heating value and gives off large amounts of soot as it burns. It is sometimes recycled to provide heat for coking. It is possible to make high-energy gas and liquid fuels, such as gasoline and fuel oil, from coal, but this is a costly and complex process.

■ This coking plant is in Pennsylvania.

DISCOVERING PETROLEUM

The word *petroleum* comes from two Latin words meaning "rock oil." People have been using oil from rocks for thousands of years. The ancient Egyptians coated mummies with pitch, a sticky black substance made from coal tar. Pitch is obtained from bituminous coal. Pitch was also used in ancient times to make wooden ships watertight. Centuries before European settlers arrived, Native Americans used crude oil for fuel and to make medicine. In the eastern United States, the remains of oil wells indicate that Native Americans knew how to get oil from underground deposits.

By the mid-18th century, North American colonists had found many oil seepages around New York, Pennsylvania, and West Virginia. Some wells that were dug for salt produced oil, which was regarded as a nuisance. In the 1840s, Abraham Gesner, a Canadian **geologist**, discovered kerosene. With the growing popularity of this fuel, which could be obtained from coal or oil, oil became more valuable.

Birth of the oil industry

In 1859 Edwin L. Drake, a former railroad conductor, drilled a well near Titusville, Pennsylvania. People called it Drake's Folly, not believing that he would find anything. However, Drake struck oil. Wooden **derricks** sprang up all over the hills of Pennsylvania as other prospectors began to drill wells nearby. Within three years, so much oil was being produced that the price of a barrel fell from $20 to 10 cents. To begin with, wagons and river barges carried the oil to refineries, but soon railroad lines had to be laid to the oil fields to transport the growing quantities of oil. In 1865 the first successful oil pipeline was built to carry oil 5 miles (8 kilometers) from Titusville to the nearest railroad link. Within ten years, a 62-mile (100-kilometer) pipe took oil to Pittsburgh.

■ Drake's oil well was in Titusville, Pennsylvania.

The industry grows

In 1860 Italy became the next country to produce oil, followed by Canada, Poland, Russia, Venezuela, Indonesia, Mexico, and several other countries. The first oil fields of the Middle East were discovered in Iran in 1908, in Iraq in 1927, and in Saudi Arabia in 1938.

At first, kerosene was the chief product of the petroleum industry. Gasoline was just a useless by-product that was dumped away, often straight into rivers. At the beginning of the 20th century, this changed with the arrival of electric lights and the automobile. Suddenly, gasoline was not useless anymore. The introduction of the thermal-cracking process in 1913 meant that the larger hydrocarbon molecules present in petroleum could be split into smaller gasoline molecules. This boosted the amount of gasoline that could be obtained from crude oil from eleven barrels of gasoline out of every hundred barrels of crude oil to well over twenty barrels.

World War I (1914–18) saw a huge increase in demand for petroleum fuels to power ships, trains, trucks, and aircraft. After the war, many more farmers in the United States and Europe began to use tractors and other oil-powered equipment. World War II (1939–45) caused another huge increase in the production of petroleum, because more oil products were needed for fuels and lubricants. After the war, the demand for petroleum products kept on growing.

■ Supplies of petroleum were important for the armed forces in World War II.

NATURAL GAS

Natural gas is easily distributed through pipelines and can be used for a wide variety of purposes, such as heating and cooking in homes and businesses. It has several advantages over other fuels. It can be quickly lit and put out just as quickly, and it can be burned in large or small amounts. This allows people to make small temperature adjustments. In comparison to coal and oil, natural gas produces much less pollution when burned.

Finding natural gas

Natural gas forms beneath Earth's surface over millions of years as part of the same process that forms petroleum. This means that oil and natural gas are often found together. The natural gas is on top of the oil deposit or is dissolved in it.

Natural gas is found in porous rocks such as limestone and sandstone. A dome of **nonporous** rock, such as a **salt dome**, forms a cap over the gas-bearing rock and traps the gas. The gas cannot escape until a drill opens a hole through the solid rock.

Drilling for gas is done the same way as drilling for oil. The most common method is **rotary** drilling. **Offshore** gas wells are drilled in water as much as 1,500 feet (2,400 meters) deep. Offshore drillers work from a barge, a movable rig, or a fixed platform. Offshore drilling costs more than drilling on land, but it is usually much more productive. Some of the richest offshore gas-producing areas are the Gulf Coast waters off the United States and the North Sea around Europe.

■ A crew drilling for natural gas fits drill pipes together.

The gas industry

The natural gas industry began in the United States. It grew quickly in the late 1920s with the development of improved pipes that could carry gas long distances cheaply. Up until the 1960s, little natural gas was available in Europe. But, with the discovery of gas fields in the North Sea and in the former Soviet Union, the natural gas industry expanded rapidly. The world's largest known gas field was found in the Soviet Union in 1966.

Gas distribution

Natural gas has to be cleaned and treated when it leaves the well. It is first taken to an extraction unit, where impurities are removed. Next, it may be taken to processing plants, where butane, propane, and ethane can be taken out. The processed natural gas is then fed under high pressure into underground transmission pipelines to consumers. The pressure of the gas drops as it is used up and because of friction against the pipe walls. Compressor stations build the pressure up again.

EXPLOSIVE POWER

In 1967 a hydrogen bomb with an explosive power equivalent to over 28,500 tons of TNT was detonated 4,265 feet (1,300 meters) underground in the San Juan Basin of northwestern New Mexico. The explosion made gas deposits available that had been trapped in rock formations. These formations had been too hard for normal drilling.

Gas mains are large pipes connected to the transmission pipelines. Smaller pipes, called service lines, branch off from the mains, carrying the gas to consumers in homes, factories, schools, and other buildings. Because pure natural gas has no odor, a chemical is added to make it smell. This makes gas leaks more noticeable.

■ This drilling rig is in the gas fields of the Gulf of Mexico.

WORKING IN A COAL MINE

Thousands of miners—men, women, and children—have been killed in mine accidents. Many thousands have died of lung diseases as a result of breathing in coal dust. All early large-scale mining was done by hand, using picks and bars to remove the coal from the solid rock. In the 19th century, when demand for coal was soaring, many miners worked underground for over ten hours a day, six days a week. Once the coal was removed, it was hauled to the surface by humans or animals such as dogs, ponies, and horses.

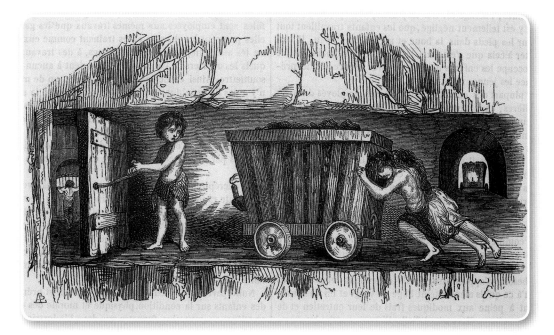

■ Children as young as ten wheeled coal from mines in the 19th century.

In the late 18th century, miners started using explosives to blast the coal. In the late 18th and the 19th centuries, steam power was used to transport coal and to pump water from mines. This greatly improved underground coal mining. Today, most of the work in coal mines is carried out using machines. Although safety has been improved, coal mining is still dangerous.

Modern methods

There are three main ways to reach an underground coal seam. If a seam is exposed to the surface, on the side of a hill or mountain, a mine can be dug directly into the coal seam. This is the easiest and least expensive method. Otherwise, an inclined opening is dug through the surrounding rock to reach the coal seam, or a vertical mine shaft is dug down to the seam. Once the seam has been reached, a variety of methods are used to get the coal out.

In conventional mining, the coal is first cut using a large chainsaw on wheels called an undercutter. Explosives are put into holes drilled into the coal. They blast the coal from the seam. The coal is then loaded into a shuttle car that takes it to a conveyor belt for transportation to the surface. Roof support for the mine is provided by wooden timbers, steel beams set on posts, or steel rods anchored into holes drilled in the roof.

The continuous mining system uses a single machine that does the job of the undercutter, drills, explosives, and loading machine. Other machines include the boring machine, which cuts or breaks the coal using arms that rotate against the coal face. A ripper, which is similar to an undercutter, cuts the coal using chains on the coal face and can load the coal that it cuts. A milling or drum miner cuts the coal with drill bits mounted on rotating drums that are vertically parallel to the coal face. Drum miners are widely used today.

STRIP MINING

Strip mining, or surface mining, began in about 1910, when steam shovels were first being used. Today, 60 percent of all coal is mined by this method. Often the coal deposit is covered by soil, which must first be stripped off, usually by large machines, such as bucket-wheel excavators. The coal is then broken up by explosives.

In longwall mining, large exposed blocks of coal are removed. **Hydraulic jacks** provide roof support. These jacks advance as the coal is mined and the roof behind the jacks collapses. A conveyor belt transports the broken coal to the surface.

■ No matter how sophisticated the equipment, mining is still dangerous.

SEARCHING FOR OIL

Before about 1900, oil prospectors drilled where they found an oil seepage and hoped for the best. Their equipment was little more than a pick, a shovel, and perhaps a divining rod. (A divining rod is a forked stick that some believed would magically lead them to the right place.) In the 20th century, however, oil exploration became more of a science, as geologists built up an understanding of how and why oil deposits are formed.

Oil and geology

Oil geologists try to find oil by studying rock formations. First, they select an area that might be promising—for example, where there are sedimentary rocks. Next, they make a detailed map of the area using photographs from satellites and aircraft and observations they carried out on the ground. They study the map for signs of possible oil traps. A low bulge might be caused by a salt dome, one common type of petroleum trap.

■ A 19th-century engraving shows men being swamped by a gusher as Drake's Folly strikes oil.

The next stage is to take cores, which are cylindrical samples cut through the layers of rock in an area. The geologists examine the structure and chemical make-up of the core. **Geophysicists** can locate geological structures that may contain oil with the aid of special instruments, such as gravimeters, magnetometers, and seismographs.

The gravimeter, or **gravity** meter, measures the pull of gravity at a particular location. Different kinds of rocks have different effects on gravity—for example, nonporous rocks tend to increase gravitational pull, while porous rocks tend to decrease it. Low readings on a gravimeter might indicate the presence of porous rocks, such as sandstone, that could contain oil.

A magnetometer measures changes in Earth's **magnetic field**. The magnetic field, like gravity, is affected by the type of rocks beneath the surface. Sedimentary rocks usually have weaker magnetic fields than other types of rock. This difference allows potentially oil-bearing sedimentary rocks to be identified.

Seismographic surveys

A seismograph measures the speed of vibrations traveling through Earth, either from an earthquake or from an underground explosion. Geophysicists can map the depth and shape of many potential oil traps by recording the changing speed of the vibrations as they travel through rocks. To avoid using explosives to produce vibrations, geophysicists will sometimes use a thumper truck, which strikes the ground repeatedly with a large metal plate.

Geologists also carry out seismographic surveys at sea. A pulse of compressed air or an electronic pulse is sent out from a ship into the water. The waves from this pulse are reflected back from underwater features and are recorded.

Seismographs allow geologists to look for fluids, such as oil or gas, in rock formations under the ground by using a technique called bright spot technology. Highly sensitive recorders pick up changes in the height of the vibration waves as they are reflected from rocks that contain fluids. These variations appear as bright spots on the wave patterns recorded by the seismograph.

■ Thumper trucks got their name because they "thump" the ground to create artificial vibrations. Here, they search for oil in the desert of Libya.

DRILLING FOR OIL

No matter how thoroughly geologists survey an area, there is still only one chance in ten that oil is actually found when the drilling begins, and only one chance in fifty that it will be there in amounts to justify the cost of removing it.

Preparing the site

A drilling site on land is first of all leveled and cleared with bulldozers. Roads are built to transport personnel and heavy equipment to the site. Supplies of water and power are provided, along with living quarters for the workforce if there are no towns nearby. The oil rig, which consists mainly of drilling equipment and a derrick, will arrive by truck, barge, or aircraft, depending on the accessibility of the site.

Rigging up

Connecting the parts of the oil rig is called rigging up. First, the construction crew builds the derrick over the spot where the well is to be drilled. Derricks range in height from 75 to 195 feet (24 to 60 meters), depending on how deep the oil is believed to be. Then, workers attach hoisting machinery, which raises and lowers the drill in and out of the well hole, to the derrick. Next, workers install the engines that power the drill and other machinery on the rig, as well as a variety of pipes, tanks, pumps, and other equipment. After workers attach the drill to the hoisting machinery, they can start to dig the well hole.

Drilling

In cable-tool drilling, a steel cable repeatedly raises and drops a heavy cutting tool called a bit. Each time the bit drops, it cuts deeper into the ground. This method is best suited to digging shallow wells into hard rock. Bits may be over 1.2 feet (2 meters) in length and over 12 inches (30 centimeters) in diameter. Every so often, workers remove the cable and drill bit and pour water into the hole. They scoop out the water and particles at the bottom of the hole using a long steel pipe called a bailer.

In rotary drilling, workers attach a bit to the end of a series of connected pipes, called the drill pipe. As the drill pipe is lowered into the ground, it is rotated, and the bit cuts into the rock.

Different bits are used for hard and soft rocks. As the hole becomes deeper, extra lengths of pipe can be added. Drilling mud is pumped down the drill pipe. It flows out of the openings in the bit and back up between the pipe and the wall of the hole. This mud cools and cleans the bit and also carries soil and rock from the drill hole to the surface. The pressure of the mud in the well reduces the risk of blowouts and gushers, which are caused by the sudden release of pressure in an oil reservoir. Blowouts and gushers waste oil and may even destroy the rig.

■ Workers add piping to an oil well in Wyoming.

CHANGING THE BIT

The drilling crew changes the bit when it becomes dull or if a different type is needed. To change the bit, they must pull out the entire drill pipe, which may be more than 25,000 feet (7,600 meters) long.

OFFSHORE OPERATIONS

Offshore oil explorations are much more difficult and dangerous than drilling operations on land. Crew and equipment must be transported to the site by helicopter or ship. In waters such as the North Sea and the Arctic Ocean, oil rigs may be damaged by storms or ice. On average, it costs ten times more to set up an offshore rig than to construct one on land. About one-third of the world's oil comes from offshore oil fields.

Drilling offshore

Drilling an offshore well is similar to drilling a well on land. The parts of the drilling rig are the same, but the rig must be mounted on something that can be taken to sea. Wells drilled to explore a site are placed on movable rigs, such as jack-up rigs and semi-submersible rigs, or on drill ships. When oil has been found and a well comes into production, a fixed platform is used.

JACK-UP RIGS: Jack-up rigs are commonly used in depths of up to 46 feet (60 meters), although they can be used in up to 360 feet (110 meters) of water. Jack-up rigs get their name because they sit on a floating platform attached to steel legs that can be jacked up or down. When the rig is moved, the legs are jacked up off the seafloor, the platform is lowered into the water, and boats tow it to a new site. Once in position, the legs are lowered to the seafloor again, and the platform is raised above the surface.

SEMI-SUBMERSIBLE RIGS: Semi-submersible rigs are used to explore for oil in depths of up to 3,900 feet (1,200 meters). The rig is mounted on a pontoon suspended just beneath the surface of the ocean. Anchors hold the rig in position.

■ Drill ships use satellite navigation to stay in position over a deep-water well site.

DRILL SHIPS: Drill ships are used in water up to 7,900 feet (2,400 meters) deep. The derrick and other drilling equipment are mounted on the deck of the drill ship, and the drill pipe is lowered through an opening in the bottom of the ship. Onboard computers take readings from navigation satellites and make small adjustments using the ship's engines to maintain a precise position over the drilling site.

Production platforms

Production platforms are only built and put in position after explorations have uncovered a reserve of oil large enough to justify the cost. Most fixed platforms are used in shallow water, but they can be used in depths of 980 feet (300 meters) or more.

Production platforms are built in segments that are taken to the drilling site in barges. The bottom segment is guided and lowered to the seafloor with cranes and secured to the seafloor with giant stakes, called piles. A second segment is fitted on top of the bottom segment. Some production platforms have three segments. The top segment is the base for the drilling operations. More than 40 wells can be drilled in various directions from a production platform.

■ An oil production platform in the North Sea burns off excess gas from the well.

OIL STRIKE!

Drilling for oil is expensive and time-consuming. Throughout the drilling operations, the riggers (crew of a rig) look carefully for evidence of petroleum in the pieces of rock brought up by the drilling mud. When the riggers reach a depth likeliest to hold an oil deposit, they carry out further tests.

Testing for oil

Coring involves replacing the drill bit (cutting tool) with a coring bit. A coring bit cuts out a cylinder of rock that can be brought up to the surface for analysis. Another test involves lowering measuring instruments, called sondes, into the well hole. They provide information about the composition, fluid content, and other features of the underground rock. Riggers will also take samples of fluids and measure their pressure in the drill hole. If they find no evidence of oil, the well may be plugged with cement and abandoned.

Casing

If the crew finds a productive well, they remove the drill pipe and lower steel casing (a steel pipe) into the well hole. They pump wet cement down the casing and cover it with a special plug that can be drilled through. While the cement is still wet, they pump mud into the casing and push the plug to the bottom. They force the cement up from the bottom of the hole to the surface, filling the space between the well hole and the outside of the casing. Once the cement has hardened, the riggers can continue drilling through the plug.

■ Riggers in China work to control a gushing oil well.

The steel casing acts as a protective lining for the well hole, helping to prevent leaks and the possible collapse of the hole. At the top of the casing, the drilling crew fits a blowout preventer. This is a giant valve that closes off the casing if pressure builds in the well.

Coming into production

Bringing the well into production is carried out in several steps. First, the crew lowers an instrument called a perforator into the casing. When it reaches the depth where the oil has been found, the perforator fires explosive charges into the casing. It punches holes through which the oil can enter. Next, the crew installs tubing. This is a string of smaller pipes that conducts the oil to the surface. The casing itself would be too wide to get the oil flowing up fast enough. Tubing is also easier to repair and replace than the steel casing.

■ Valves control the flow of lubricants to a North Sea oil rig.

Finally, the crew puts together a group of control valves at the upper end of the casing and tubing to control the flow of oil to the surface. Because of its many branch-like fittings, this valve assembly is known as a Christmas tree. More than one oil-bearing zone may be found where a well has been drilled. In this case, the crew will install separate tubing and control valves for each zone.

POWER STATIONS

It is hard to imagine life without electricity. Electricity heats and lights our homes and provides power for our computers, televisions, refrigerators, and a variety of other appliances. Machinery in factories, offices, and hospitals also relies on electric power. Virtually all the electricity we use is produced by huge electricity generators in power stations. Most of these power stations are burning fossil fuels (coal, oil, or natural gas) to operate the generators. Fossil-fuel power stations generate over 60 percent of the world's electric power.

Superheated steam power

In power stations, fuel is burned in a combustion chamber to produce heat. This heat is used to convert water to steam in a boiler. The steam flows through a set of tubes in a device called a superheater. The temperature and pressure of the steam in the tubes is raised by surrounding the superheater with hot gases from the combustion chamber.

The superheated, high-pressure steam is used to drive a huge steam turbine. A steam turbine consists of a series of wheels, each with many fan-like blades, mounted on a central shaft. As the steam flows through the turbine, it pushes against the blades, causing both the wheels and the turbine shaft to spin. The spinning shaft turns the rotor of an electricity generator.

■ This electricity generator is inside a coal-burning power station.

An electricity generator has two main parts: a stationary part called a stator and a rotating part called a rotor. In the massive generators used in power stations, the stator consists of hundreds of coils of copper wire. The rotor is a large **electromagnet**. As the spinning shaft of the turbine turns the rotor, the magnetic field created by the rotor turns as the rotor turns. This spinning magnetic field produces a **voltage** in the wire coils of the stator, causing an electric current to flow.

After the steam leaves the turbine, it passes into a condenser. There, it flows around pipes carrying cool water. The heat from the steam is transferred to the water in the pipes and the steam cools, condenses into water again, and is pumped back to the boiler in the furnace.

Spray ponds and cooling towers

The water in the condenser pipes, which has absorbed heat from the steam, has to be cooled before it can be used again. To do this, the heated water is pumped to a spray pond or a cooling tower. At a spray pond, the water is sprayed out through nozzles. This increases its surface area and therefore increases the rate at which it loses heat to the

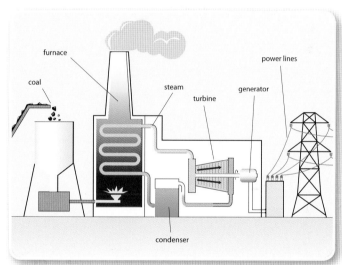

■ Coal is burned to heat water, which produces steam, which spins a turbine, which turns a generator, which produces our electricity!

surrounding air. In a cooling tower, the water spills down through a series of decks, cooling as it comes into contact with the air. The cooled water may be recycled through the condenser or simply discharged into a nearby lake or river or into the sea.

POLLUTION PROBLEMS

Fossil-fuel power stations are a reliable way to produce huge amounts of electrical energy, but they are not without their problems. Some power plants release heated water into the environment, which may harm plant and animal life. Also, the smoke from burning fossil fuels causes air pollution.

MOVING THE WORLD

We depend on the internal combustion engine to power all the cars and trucks in the world. A combustion engine burns a mixture of fuel and air, turning chemical energy into heat energy. The heat energy is then converted into **mechanical energy** to perform useful work.

Gasoline engines

The most common kind of internal combustion engine is the gasoline-powered **piston** engine, which uses gasoline taken from petroleum. The rate at which a gasoline engine produces work is usually measured in horsepower or watts. Gasoline engines are well suited for powering vehicles because they are compact and lightweight for the power they produce.

There are two main types of gasoline engine: reciprocating engines and rotary engines. Reciprocating engines have pistons that move up and down or back and forth. A crankshaft converts this reciprocating motion into rotary, or revolving, motion. A rotary engine—also known as a Wankel engine, after its inventor, Ferdinand Wankel—uses rotors instead of pistons. The rotors produce rotary motion directly.

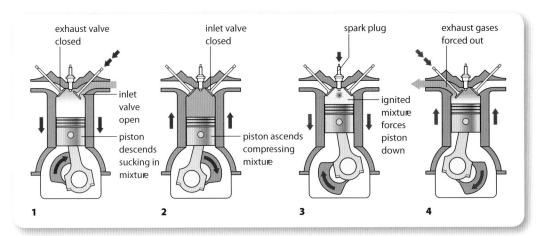

■ This is the process by which an internal combustion engine works.

HYBRID CARS

Today, there are environmentally friendly alternatives to gasoline- or diesel-powered cars. One of these is the hybrid car. This type of car can use batteries for driving in crowded areas and a gasoline engine for long-distance journeys. Hybrid cars have smaller engines than normal cars, so they are more fuel-efficient.

Car engines

Most car engines consist of several cylinders arranged in one or two rows, each containing a piston and a spark plug. A mixture of air and gasoline is forced into the cylinder and compressed. Then, a spark from the spark plug explodes the gasoline mix, pushing the piston along the cylinder. The pistons are connected to a rod, called a crankshaft. As a piston slides down the cylinder, it makes the crankshaft turn. The engine is set up so that the pistons are fired down the cylinders one after another. In this way, the crankshaft keeps turning. The crankshaft is connected to the wheels of the car through a series of gears, which makes the wheels turn as the crankshaft turns. The amount of power the engine produces is controlled by a throttle that regulates how much air and fuel enter the cylinder.

Diesel engines

Diesel engines are mainly used for heavy-duty work, such as powering trains, large freight trucks, and buses, although some cars also use diesel engines. Diesel power is also used in ships and submarines and in emergency electricity generators. Diesel engines are larger and heavier than gasoline engines of equivalent power.

■ Diesel engines are often used to provide the power for large trucks.

They burn fuel oils that, like gasoline, are obtained from petroleum. However, the fuel oils require less refining and are cheaper to produce. The diesel engine compresses the air in the cylinders, causing the air temperature to rise. Fuel is then injected into the hot, compressed air and ignites immediately. As with a gasoline engine, the resulting explosion pushes against pistons, forcing them along cylinders to turn a crankshaft.

NEAR-DEATH EXPERIENCE

The diesel engine was invented by Rudolf Diesel, a German engineer who patented his design in 1892 and built his first engine in 1893. The engine exploded and almost killed him.

FOSSIL-FUELED FLIGHT

Aircraft use two main types of engines: reciprocating engines and jet engines, both of which use fossil fuels.

Piston power

Reciprocating engines, also called piston engines, are the most widely used type of airplane engine. Although not as powerful as jet engines, they are still used in most light aircraft because they are more efficient at low speeds. The engine burns a fine spray of gasoline and air inside cylinders, using the explosion to drive pistons inside the cylinders up and down and to rotate a crankshaft. In an aircraft, the rotating crankshaft turns the propeller, whereas in a car it makes the wheels spin.

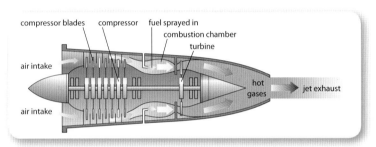

■ This is a cross-section of a jet engine.

Jet power

The principle of jet propulsion was first described in 1687 by Sir Isaac Newton in his third law of motion. This law states that for every action, there is an equal and opposite reaction. It is simply demonstrated by blowing up a balloon and releasing it. The air escaping from the balloon's neck is the action. The equal and opposite reaction is the wayward flight of the balloon around the room. Jet propulsion drives an aircraft engine in much the same way. Gas pressure inside the engine is produced by burning fuel in a combustion chamber. Most jet engines use a liquid petroleum fuel similar to kerosene. The gases are directed out through a nozzle as a powerful stream of jet exhaust that pushes the engine forward.

THE SKY'S THE LIMIT

In recent years, there has been a huge increase in air travel. Many people are concerned about the effects this increase will have on the environment. This is due not only to using more land for new airports, but also to the increased levels of carbon dioxide emissions. About 13 percent of global transportation-related emissions come from air travel.

Jet engines weigh less than reciprocating engines, but they produce much greater power. This enables large aircraft to travel long distances at high speeds. There are three main types: turbojets; turbofans, or fanjets; and turboprops.

TURBOJET: A turbojet takes air in through the front and burns it with fuel to give a powerful jet exhaust. This thrusts the aircraft forward. As the jet exhaust passes out through the engine's tail pipe, it spins a turbine that turns a compressor, raising the pressure of the air in the engine. The turbojet was the first successful jet engine, and it is still used today.

TURBOFANS: A turbofan operates in a similar way to a turbojet, but it has a fan at the front that draws in air. Part of the air sucked in by the fan is burned with the fuel and the rest is added to the exhaust as it passes from the tail pipe. This results in an exhaust that is much cooler than that of a turbojet, but at the same time more powerful. Turbofans are more efficient at low speeds, are quieter, and use less fuel than turbojets. Almost all new commercial passenger jets have turbofan engines.

■ The fossil-fuel burning jet engine has revolutionized world transportation.

TURBOPROPS: A turboprop, as the name suggests, is a combination of a turbojet and a propeller. The turboprop is basically a turbojet that uses its power to spin a power turbine, which turns a propeller. The energy left in the combustion gases, after they have turned the power turbine, adds a small amount of jet thrust to the propeller's thrust. A turboprop combines the power of a jet engine and the stability of a propeller aircraft. Turboprops are smaller and lighter than piston engines, but they produce the same amount of power.

GAS GUZZLERS!

A Boeing 747 can fly for 6,000 miles (9,700 kilometers) on a single load of fuel (39,000 gallons, or 178,000 liters). This works out to just under 6.5 miles per gallon (18 liters per kilometer)!

THE ENVIRONMENTAL IMPACT

Removing fossil fuels from the ground and transporting them to wherever they are needed damages the environment. In strip mining (see page 21), earth-moving machines gouge holes in the ground, sometimes many miles across, to get at coal seams. Waste materials, called spoils, tend to produce acids when they are exposed to rain. Run-off from the strip mines may pollute nearby waterways when rainwater mixed with the acids runs down the bare slopes. This run-off washes away fertile soils. Strip mining also results in fertile soil being buried under tons of rock. Waste material from deep shaft mines has to be dumped on land or in the sea.

Strip-mined land can be reclaimed by leveling the steep slopes formed by the spoils and replacing as much topsoil as possible. This allows the area to be replanted.

Sometimes mines can settle. Removing large seams of coal from under the ground causes the layers of rock above the coal seam to collapse, leading to damage to buildings, roads, and underground pipes and cables. Agriculture can also be affected when drainage systems are disrupted.

In their search for petroleum, oil companies must build roads and temporary structures in places where there might be oil. In the United States, for example, a great deal of controversy has been caused by oil exploration in the delicate **ecosystem** of the Arctic tundra. Leaks from wells drilled in shallow coastal waters create oil slicks that pollute beaches and kill sea life.

■ The biggest mines in the world are strip mines where minerals lie near the surface.

Oil spills

In December 1999, the 25-year-old tanker *Erika* broke in two, spilling more than 11,000 tons of fuel oil on French beaches. This is just one of a number of incidents in which coastlines have been badly polluted by oil spills.

The U.S. government enacted the Oil Pollution Act (OPA) in 1990 after the *Exxon Valdez* oil spill caused huge environmental damage in Alaska. This legislation demands the use of double-hulled vessels, which are believed to reduce the chances of pollution in low-impact collisions or groundings. Operators have been given until 2015 to upgrade their fleets.

In Europe, single-hull crude tankers above a certain weight will not be able to enter European ports after January 1, 2010, if proposed regulations become law. Although all new tankers have been built with double hulls since 1996, the new regulations would still make up to 50 percent of ships unusable.

■ Volunteers begin the difficult task of cleaning up after an oil spill on the coast of France.

OIL SPILLS WAITING TO HAPPEN?

More than 2.2 billion tons of crude and refined oil products were transported globally by sea in 1998.

POLLUTION AND CLIMATE CHANGE

The major sources of air pollution are cars, trucks, buses, factories, and fossil fuel power stations. Air pollution contaminates the air with chemicals that can cause damage to ecosystems, are dangerous to people's health, and generally make life less pleasant.

Acid rain

Acid rain is caused when chemicals released into the air from vehicle exhaust and from coal-burning power stations dissolve in water in the atmosphere to form sulfuric and nitric acids. This makes rain, snow, and fog more acidic than usual. Air currents can carry the acid many miles away from the site of the pollution before it falls and damages crops, trees, lakes, and buildings.

Many lakes in the northeastern United States, Canada, and Scandinavia are so acidic that fish can no longer live there. Acid rain can turn buildings and statues black and damage them by corroding metal, stone, and paint. Monuments and statues that have survived erosion by the weather for hundreds of years are suddenly being eaten away.

The greenhouse effect

Earth's atmosphere contains gases called greenhouse gases. In a real greenhouse, the Sun's rays pass through the glass, but its heat energy cannot pass back out. Greenhouse gases work in a similar way. They let the Sun's rays pass through to the surface of the planet, but they prevent the heat reflected back from Earth's surface from being radiated into space. As a result, the atmosphere gradually warms up.

■ These trees in Poland have been damaged by acid rain.

Carbon dioxide, a greenhouse gas, is present naturally in the atmosphere. However, burning fossil fuels also produces carbon dioxide. Carbon dioxide trapped beneath the ground in coal and oil reserves is now being released into the atmosphere at an enormous rate. About 7.7 billion tons of carbon dioxide from burning fossil fuels and deforestation are released annually. Natural processes, such as the absorption of carbon dioxide by trees, removes about half of this, but the remaining 3.85 billion tons remain in the atmosphere for 50 to 200 years. Therefore, the amount of carbon dioxide in the atmosphere keeps increasing.

Many scientists believe that rising levels of carbon dioxide and other greenhouse gases are causing Earth's climate to become warmer. This effect is called global warming. As a result, the climate could become so warm that some of the polar ice caps melt, causing the sea level to rise. Also, the water in the oceans will expand as it is heated. Many coastal settlements will then be flooded. The worst effects of global warming could bring devastating floods and storms to many parts of the world as weather patterns are altered. Such changes are unpredictable.

■ Heavy traffic in Mexico City causes a lot of pollution.

Many countries are working to reduce air pollution—for example, through the development of vehicles that are more fuel efficient and so burn less gasoline. More power stations and factories are installing filters on their smokestacks to trap harmful chemicals before they can enter the atmosphere.

NONRENEWABLE RESOURCES

Fossil fuels are nonrenewable resources. This means that once our stocks have been used up, they cannot be replaced in the foreseeable future. As we have seen, the formation of fossil fuels is a continuing process, but it takes many millions of years to get from plant and animal life to coal, petroleum, and natural gas. We are using these resources much faster than natural processes are replacing them. The world relies very heavily on fossil fuels, and a great deal of effort will have to be made to find alternatives. Ordinary people can play a part, too, by saving energy. If we use less electricity, less coal will have to be burned to produce it. If we walk or cycle instead of driving cars everywhere, less gasoline will be consumed, pollution will be cut down, and resources will be conserved.

Crisis? What crisis?

During the oil crisis of the 1970s (see pages 42–43), there was panic as people began to believe that the oil supplies were running dry and prices would spiral up forever. Between 1973 and 1998, world oil consumption rose by around 25 percent, to 26 billion barrels annually. At the same time, proven oil reserves—those reserves of oil available at existing prices and using existing technology—jumped more than 50 percent, to one trillion barrels.

One reason for this is a huge improvement in the technology used to find oil reserves. For example, computers can make three-dimensional seismic maps of underground formations, thereby improving the chances of finding oil. That way, riggers drill fewer "dry holes" than before. The development of horizontal

drilling techniques means that more oil can be recovered from known fields. A traditional vertically drilled hole taps an oil reservoir at only one spot, from top to bottom, while a

■ A technician uses a computer to analyze data that could help pinpoint the location of an oil field.

horizontal drill can run along the length of a reservoir, allowing the oil to be removed more efficiently. Improvements in deep-water drilling techniques have opened new fields for exploration, because oil companies can now drill in waters five times deeper than a few years ago.

Coal

Coal supplies are not under quite as much pressure as oil supplies. Coal remains an important resource, providing one-quarter of the world's commercial energy needs. At current rates of production and consumption, the world's coal reserves should last for more than 200 years. Oil reserves, on the other hand, are expected to begin to run out in 40 years. Also, unlike oil, which is concentrated in the hands of a few major producers, coal reserves are evenly spread across the U.S., Europe, and Asia.

■ A train carries a fresh supply of coal to a power station.

China, for example, has very large coal reserves. However, most of these are in the northern provinces, while demand for energy is growing fastest in the south. Because it is difficult to transport coal by land, China actually has to import about 55 million tons of coal a year. Australia is one of the world's largest exporters of high-quality coal. Recently, big companies from the United States, Great Britain, and South Africa have been buying shares in Australian coal-mining businesses.

ENERGY ALTERNATIVES

As fossil fuel reserves inevitably begin to run out, scientists and engineers are exploring renewable energy sources that might take their place. These include solar energy, wind power, wave power, hydroelectric power, and geothermal energy.

FUEL WARS

Oil currently provides between 40 and 50 percent of the world's energy needs. If every nation that used oil could produce enough to meet its own needs, things would be fairly simple. However, this is not the case. Nations that consume large amounts of oil do not necessarily produce large amounts. Countries such as France and Japan, which use large amounts of oil but have no supplies of their own, have always imported their oil.

During the 1970s, the United States passed from being self-sufficient in oil to having to import more than half of its oil supplies. The so-called "oil shocks" of the time came about with the creation of the Organization of Petroleum Exporting Countries (OPEC), a group of the major oil-producing nations, which did not include Mexico, the United States, or the former Soviet Union.

OPEC takes control

In the 1960s, the OPEC countries had begun to take over the control of their own oil production from private oil companies. In the early 1970s, OPEC raised prices on crude oil to levels that affected the economies of all oil-importing countries, especially developing countries. Oil-dependent economies, such as Japan, faced economic slumps. Higher prices for petroleum-based fertilizers meant that the cost of food production rose as well. Because developed countries were paying higher prices for oil imports, they had less money to spend on importing goods from developing countries. At the same time, the developing nations had to pay more for imported goods because the cost of manufacturing rose with the increase in energy prices.

■ At the first sign of an energy crisis, motorists tend to buy in panic, putting pressure on fuel reserves.

The effects that energy has had on the world economy show how dependent we are on maintaining our supplies of it. Because coal reserves are much larger and more widely distributed than petroleum reserves, it seems unlikely that any organization could control coal production in the same way that OPEC controls the oil supply. However, increased use of coal will cause severe pollution problems.

A volatile situation

In 1998 oil prices dropped by about 50 percent. An economic crisis in Asia slowed demand, while a mild winter in the United States had the same effect. Misreading the signs, OPEC increased production and found that it had far more oil than people wanted. In the United States, exploration and drilling projects were postponed or stopped altogether and 65,000 people lost their jobs. Other oil-producing nations also suffered huge losses.

In March 1999 OPEC cut output by 1.7 million barrels a day. Four non-OPEC nations (Mexico, Russia, Norway, and Oman) also agreed to cut their combined output by 400,000 barrels a day. Demand for oil improved as Asia recovered from its economic crisis.

■ The oil fields of Kuwait were devastated by retreating Iraqi troops at the end of the Gulf War in 1991.

The problem for planners in the industrialized nations is that two-thirds of the world's known oil reserves lie in the Middle East—a region known for its unpredictable politics. Who knows what future upheavals could disrupt the flow of fuel to the developed world?

FUEL ALTERNATIVES

Japan is less dependent on oil supplies than it was in the 1970s. More than one-third of Japan's electricity is now supplied by nuclear reactors, compared with just 6.5 percent during the 1970s oil crisis. Cleaner industries such as computer software development are growing, while oil-demanding manufacturing industries, such as steel, are less important.

FOSSIL FUEL STATISTICS

World energy production

Energy is measured in joules. A joule is a small unit, and so energy is usually measured in kilojoules (thousands of joules) or larger. In the following tables, figures are given in terajoules (tJ). One terajoule is one trillion joules. A bolt of lightning unleashes around 0.003 terajoules of energy.

ENERGY PRODUCTION, 1998

United States	76.6 million tJ
Russia	41.9 million tJ
China	39.5 million tJ
Saudi Arabia	21.5 million tJ
Canada	18.2 million tJ
Great Britain	12.1 million tJ

ENERGY CONSUMPTION, 1998

United States	98.5 million tJ
China	39 million tJ
Russia	27.4 million tJ
Japan	22.6 million tJ
Germany	15.2 million tJ
Canada	12.9 million tJ
Great Britain	10.6 million tJ

COUNTRIES WITH GREATEST OIL PRODUCTION, 2004

(in million barrels per day)	
Saudi Arabia	10.37
Russia	9.27
United States	8.69
Iran	4.09

(Source: U.S. Energy Information Administration)

COUNTRIES WITH GREATEST NATURAL GAS PRODUCTION, 2004

(in billion cubic meters per year)

Russia	589.1
United States	542.9
Canada	182.8
Great Britain	95.9

(Source: U.S. Energy Information Administration)

FIND OUT MORE

If you want to learn more about fossil fuels, there is plenty of information on the Internet and in books. Use a search engine such as www.google.com to search for information. A search for the words *fossil fuels* will bring back lots of results, but it may be difficult to find the information you want. Try refining your search to look for some of the people and things mentioned in this book, such as "OPEC" or "global warming."

More Books to Read

Lim, Cheng Puay. *Our Warming Planet*. Chicago: Raintree, 2004

McLeish, Ewan. *Energy Resources*. Chicago: Raintree, 2002.

Saunders, Nigel, and Steven Chapman. *Fossil Fuel*. Chicago: Raintree, 2005.

GLOSSARY

acid rain   rain made acidic due to the presence of sulfur dioxide from coal burning and nitrogen oxides from car exhaust and other sources. These gases dissolve in the water vapor in the air, forming sulfuric and nitric acids.

atom   smallest unit of matter that can take part in a chemical reaction; the smallest part of an element that can exist

carbohydrate   major class of food, including some sugars, starches, and plant fibers

cell   smallest unit of life capable of independent existence. All living things, with the exception of viruses, consist of one or more cells.

chemical energy   energy held in the bonds that hold atoms together in molecules. Chemical energy is released during a chemical reaction.

coke   solid fuel made by heating coal in an airtight oven to remove impurities. Coke is around 90 percent carbon and is the most commonly used fuel in the iron and steel industries.

compound   chemical substance made up of two or more atoms of different elements that are bonded together

crude oil   another name for petroleum

decomposer   organism that breaks down dead matter

derrick   tower used for hoisting drill pipes

ecosystem   community of living organisms together with their non-living environment

electromagnet   magnet produced by passing an electric current through a wire wrapped around an iron core

fossil fuel   fuel produced through the action of heat and pressure on the fossil remains of plants and animals that lived millions of years ago. The fossil fuels are coal, petroleum, and natural gas.

geologist   scientist who studies the origin, history, and structure of Earth

geophysicist   scientist who studies the branch of physics concerned with Earth and its environment, including seismology (the study of earthquakes) and oceanography

geothermal   energy taken from hot rocks below Earth's surface

gravity   force of attraction between any two objects

greenhouse gas   gas in the atmosphere, such as carbon dioxide or water vapor, that absorbs heat radiated from Earth's surface that would otherwise escape into space

heat energy   energy created by moving atoms and molecules

heating value   measure of the amount of energy produced when a fuel is burned

hydraulic jacks   device powered by water pressure that is used for lifting heavy weights

impervious   something that cannot be penetrated

Industrial Revolution   period of history from around 1740 to 1850 when economic and social life was transformed by the introduction of coal-powered steam engines to drive machines for manufacturing

ion   atom that has gained or lost an electron and has an overall negative or positive charge

magnetic field region around a magnet in which a force acts on another magnet or on a moving electric charge

mechanical energy measurement of the amount of work that an object can do (a combination of the object's potential and kinetic energy)

microorganism living thing that is too small to be seen with the naked eye

mineral naturally occurring solid inorganic substance with a definite chemical composition and a characteristic structure; also used to name any substance, such as coal, that is removed from the ground

molecule two or more atoms joined together by chemical bonds. If the atoms are the same, it is an element; if they are different, it is a compound.

natural gas mainly methane, the lightest of the hydrocarbons. Other gaseous hydrocarbons found in natural gas include ethane, propane, and butane. Gases such as carbon dioxide, helium, and nitrogen may also be present.

nonporous describes a solid with few tiny holes or pores

nonrenewable resource resource that cannot be replaced after it is used up or can be replaced only over billions of years

offshore located in the ocean or sea, away from the coastline

organic describes something that is derived from living or once-living organisms

peat compacted plant remains that have partly decomposed in conditions of low oxygen

petroleum thick, yellowish-black liquid mixture of hydrocarbons found beneath the surface of Earth. It is formed by the action of bacteria and the forces of high pressure and temperature on the remains of marine plants and animals over millions of years.

photosynthesis process by which green plants and some other organisms use the energy of sunlight to make sugars from carbon dioxide and water

piston sliding piece inside an engine that is moved by fluid pressure

porous describes a solid that has many tiny holes or pores through which fluids can pass

rotary relating to rotation or spinning

salt dome underground structure formed when salt layers penetrate denser material in Earth's crust. Petroleum is often found near salt domes.

seam underground layer of a mineral such as coal

sedimentary rock rock formed over millions of years by the accumulation of layer upon layer of sediments deposited by wind, water, or ice

seepage place where petroleum seeps out of the ground

smelt obtain a metal by heating its ore (the rock from which the metal is obtained) to a high temperature

turbine engine in which a fluid is used to spin a shaft by pushing on angled blades. Turbines are used to spin electricity generators.

voltage measurement of the force that moves an electric current around a circuit

INDEX